BPP UNIVERSITY
LIBRARY AND
INFORMATION SERVICES

D1322866

To Robert, Mark, Michael, David and Christopher,

To all of my brothers
My flesh and my bone
I'm building a nest
And it's time to come home

To all of my feathers
Our flight will be soon
We're coming together
Our light is in tune

BPP UNIVERSITY
LIBRARY AND
INFORMATION SERVICES

BLACK HONEY
POETREE

Michelle Marie Clarke-Campbell

BLACK AND BEYOND BOOKS

Published by Black and Beyond Books 2004
31 Sinnington End
High Wood
Colchester
CO4 9RE

Copyright © Michelle Marie Clarke-Campbell 1995-2003
Copyright © Michelle Marie Clarke-Campbell 2004

The right of Michelle Marie Clarke-Campbell to be identified as the author of this work has been asserted by her in accordance with the Copyright, Designs and Patents Act 1988.

All rights reserved.

A CIP record for this book is available from the British Library

ISBN 0-9548458-0-3

Front cover illustrated by Stewart Campbell
Photograph title: *free little birds* © Black Honey Press

Printed in Great Britain by
Cromwell Press Limited, Trowbridge, Wiltshire.

Lord, be at the head of my table;
For it is you I serve.

For mummy, and daddy,
my sister Susan, and my sun Marcus.

I also would like to thank Stewart, Belinda, Nadia,
Melva, Lorna, and all my family and friends for their
love, support, and inspiration…

…And I thank you,

Yes, you… the one who is reading at this current moment
in time; right now we're connected

CONTENTS: Free Sevens

(21 daze in the maze)

Part Free

Step Inside

Free little Birds
Susan *(left)*, Mum *(centre)*, Michelle *(right)*

Nothing Nest

Give me some leads and I'll make some connections
And send out my signals in perfect directions

Give me some space and I'll make you some time
With stars in the face of the heaven's divine

Give me some love and I'll grant you some peace
There's always enough as it's free for release

Enter your heart and I'll guide you through life
To never depart from the true paradise

Step in the maze and I'll open your eye
On all is my gaze, be it land, sea or sky

Fly to the sun for I blessed you with wings
Believe we are one, every sweet bird that sings

This Is Man's Eternity

This is man's eternity – make it what you will
Twist and turn, uplift and yearn, and simply stand in still
This is man in lifetime and he opens like a door
He knows and grows, reveals and blows the tainted from the
pure
This is man's infinity – forever just right now
And here to say the first was day, the second shows you how
This is time in motion, and if nothing else is true
The chosen card is soft and hard to balance what we do

This is man in colour and his skin is but the shade
From pitch of night to pale as white, where stars alight have
played
This is man's own treasure; and as golden as the sand
The gift is real to touch and feel like palms within your hand
This is man's own road to tread – his heart the path to take
This is mighty natty dread with only love to make
This is of the humble and a host unto the sea
And every man will crumble to come closer to the chi

This is man's conundrum and the answer's in each peace
When winter comes to sum a man, and autumn springs
release
This is like the maze we find when no thing's really there
This is like you lose your mind to find you're in this sphere
This is like you free your soul and fly up to the sun
This is part and of the whole the kingdom is but one
This is of a higher force – and even coming down
This is never off the course and never not a round

This is quiet as a mouse when every word is read
This is from the chapter house, and every letter bread
This is man and justice, just as every man is great
No single man can crush this, though together we create
This is man in vision, and the future's in the sight
This is man's decision; many birds do not take flight

This is man's eternity; the master is a plan
And even as he turns to me and simply says – I am

Hear Me Speak

'I am everything and nothing'
The sweet birds sing –
'I am Africa! And her tortured soil
Africa! And her soothing oil
I am born out of her womb
I am deep in Egypt's tomb
I am high where pyramids peak
I am here – hear me speak'

Twinkle

I don't have the best, or what I deserve;
I live in the west and I don't know my worth
I came from the east in a ship bound for doom
I left inner peace for a trip round the moon

The stars in my eyes now appear as though pale
The sweet morning rise, in this living called hell
Surrounded by lies and my filter is loose
Drained out and dried, and when drinking the truth

Thinking is an obstacle when channels are not clear
It's deeply psychological; no ships can pass through here
How many times, how many crimes, how many more to save?
How many poor and innocent are drifting in the waves?

But every sea does know its shore and whom it comes to bless
If only for a second every single tide must rest
If only for a moment, in the twinkle of an I
A dream that's true can come for real, or fade away and die

A Part, from you

For all the times you said you love me;
When was really just a lie
For all the times you went and left your home
And me a lone to cry
For all the times the booming silence comes
Outpouring with the reign
And then for all the times of sorrow
With the solitude of shame

For all the times I came a begging
And you turned your face away
For all the times I got my leg in
Then the night was slammed on day
For all the times I rose in darkness
Just a little spark of light
For all the times you throw my heart; just
As the bird has taken flight

For all the times I tried to make it
When I didn't have a chance
And all the times you tried to break it
'Fore you even took a glance
For all the times I tried to harden;
Not to realise the cost
For all the flowers in the garden
Not afraid to just be soft

For all the times I tried to hold you
And you pushed me far and wide
For all the times you said I told you
But the truth was still denied
For all the times I tried to work it
And to form a compromise
For all the times you tried to hurt it
As it didn't suit your size
For all the times you took me sailing

Just to leave me out to sink
For all the times I'd climb the railing
Just to break the weakest link
For all the times that I was chained to you
And you weren't even there
For all the times that I explained to you
How much you didn't care

For all the times I tried to live up
To your hopes and all your dreams
For all the times I tried to give up
On what isn't as it seems
For all the times I tried to guide you
Through the karma, through the storm
So am I really here inside you?
Could you really be so torn?

Could you really be so twisted?
Could you hate yourself with scorn?
Could you really be uplifted?
In the same breath, here reborn
Could you really be a liar?
Could you really be the truth?
Are you burning in the fire;
Sitting up upon the roof?

Could you really be a healer?
Could you really be from pain?
Could you really be for real?
And yet a lion turning tame
Could you really be the power?
Is it true that you can't see?
Every second in the hour
I am you! So set me free

Un-Scene

Things are not always as they seem
The most often scene we show is the surface
Like its beautiful smile;
Yet not complete…

Sometimes one gets an inkling
To its depths; what lies beneath
Those who see deep
May catch the soul as it seeps through;
Like the sadness of its eyes
Which defies its smiles;
Completeness…

And transfers this
To an empty landscape
Where melancholic chords reign
And harmonise beauty;
Fully

And transposes this unto its
Deepness
Forever unscene
Unshown
And unreveiled

Unto it's very self; distant –
Stranger

Back to Find Me

I'm not gonna always be here;
I will be here forever
That may not somewhat seem clear
But that doesn't mean it will never

I am what I am and that won't change
But I will, I feel and I know
I'll be what I'll be and I'll be changing
Slowly with time as I grow

I inflect what I see in my own way
I protect what I feel in my needs
I reflect what I know in what I say
I inject what I am in my seeds

So many are here to remind me
So many are left in the past
My future has come back to find me
And answer each question I ask

He Told Me (Sign of Time)

He told me, you will learn in time
If only you can read the sign
He told me, please do not forget
To understand you must accept
He told me many a strange word
Silent was I when he was heard
He told me that I must tell you
He showed me what he said was true

He told me there are many here
But only few have time to spare
He told me that you must believe
All that you give you will receive
He told me there are things you see
That really were not meant to be
He told me do not close your eyes
To look inside and realise

He told me there is always choice
To hear your heart and hear his voice
He spoke and I felt peace within
I have no fear but fear of him
He told me, do not be afraid
I've come to guide the sheep that strayed
He told me, in him you can trust
Eternal is his love in us

He told me wisdom is a key
To open doors and set you free
He told me many doors have closed
And many obstacles have rose
He told me you must overcome
To learn yourself and teach the young
He said we all get what we're due
He said the world belongs to you

He told me, you were born to write
He said my words would bring you light
He sent the guitar on the wall
I answer for I hear his call
He looks through windows of the soul
There's nothing that he does not know
He told me that we all are one
There's nothing new under the sun

He told me always speak the truth
For words stand strong and stand as proof
He told me there's a sacred ground
And many seeds are homeward bound
He told me there's a special line
Of generations drawn through time
He told me we should look within
And see that we are part of him

He told me follow when you feel
For there's a way when there's a will
He told me there's no need for greed
He told me that the lambs would feed
He told me there are dangerous minds
He told me what one seeks he finds
He told me look deep in your soul
Each rainbow is a pot of gold

Everything and Nothing

I can't give you the answers to the supernatural manger
I can't give you my energy without balance exchanged
I can't lead you to freedom if you don't see your chains
I can't lead you to happiness and help to heal your pains
I can't open the mysteries if you do not know why
There are so many circles in the circle of our sky
I can't show you the place to look if you are blind to see
I can't teach you to know yourself if you do not know me

I can't give you my prophecies of all that is to come
I can not say what is to be if you are deaf and dumb
I can't give you the meanings to the feelings that you show
If you don't see you're dreaming in the places that you go
I can't give you solutions to the problems that you make
If you can't understand the simple vibe of give and take
If you can't see it's tragic when you don't know who you are
You can not see the magic I am writing on the star

I can't show you the path to take if you do not have feet
I can not teach you how to walk if we can never meet
And if I blow on broken wings and give them now to fly
Know from this moment they begin to live and also die
And if I take a broken soul and teach it how to breathe
It must then learn how to blow and who needs to receive
And if I take a broken mind and peace him back again
Everything he tries to find must lead to where I am

And if I take your broken heart and beat it like a drum
Would you hear the sound of life or would you turn and run?
And if I plant a tree of life would you see the fruit
Or would you see the side of me that's growing from the root?
Could you see salvation if it poked you in the eye?
Could I drown a nation with a river running dry?
Can I change the seasons, make the sunshine and the rain?
Know I can do everything and nothing is my name

And if I gave you paradise and everything you need
And blessed you with eternal life and whispered do not
greed
And if I fulfilled all your dreams and gave you what is pure
Would you be content with this or would you ask for more?
And if I gave you nature with her righteous balance true
Would you take good care of her or would you kill her too?
And if I gave you all you need to grow and love and live
Would you come to take from me or know it's yours to
give?

And if I gave perfection and every peaceful state
Would you rise and take the prize or take the face of hate?
And if I gave you wisdom and everything divine
And gave you power with such strength it passed the length
of time
And if I was of mercy and had forgiving ways
Would you cry and beg to me, or would you cry my praise?
And if I gave my image, with my hope, my faith, my trust
What if I gave you everything and nothing was enough?

Actions Speak Louder Than Words

She said: "Look at society! What has gone wrong?
So much anxiety, where is it from?
Look at the governments, blood on their hand
Blood in the water, the mud, and the sand
Where is the justice? Can you not see?
Why don't we stand up and fight to be free?
Why are we frightened? Who can we trust?
If we come together, they'll never beat us

Let us use unity; come as a tool
Stand up together, decide who must rule
Ours is the victory; stand in the light
Don't be the victim; children in the night
We have the power; we have it all
We are the flower that can never fall
We are the petals that can never die
We are the roots with our stem in the sky

We are the history, know yours not theirs
We are the mystery, source of their fears
We are the nation, we face them in sin
Racing relations when no one can win
We are the sheep and we keep the wrong hand
Following wolves to the alien land
We are the parents, our children we mould
Giving so little; look how much we hold"

She said: "Bring me a seed and if it is pure
I'll grow you a million flowers that cure
And if there's an illness and no remedy
It's probably manmade intentionally"
She said: "I'll teach my children right, they'll understand"
WATCHING JERRY SPRINGER, A FAG IN HER HAND
DREAMING OF PARADISE, BUT IT WON'T BE
A DOOR IS A DOOR, EVEN IF THERE'S NO KEY!

...After Thought

But every door must open, even if it's blocked
And every bee with sweet honey can open every lock

And everything's for giving and everything is here
What's the point of living if you don't know how to share

And everything is possible and all can be achieved
If you are philosophical and know how to believe

And everything is science, and everything takes time
And every man a giant if his actions are divine

For the love of money is the
root of all evil

1 Timothy, 6:10

Money Talks

'I am the beast who comes to feast
I am the crinkle, cut and crease
I take the most and break the least
I am the war who tore the peace
I am the soul who can't be saved
I am the shallow in the grave
I am the tidal in the wave
The homicidal phantom bathes

I don't have meaning, don't have worth
You give me all that I deserve
I don't exist; I'm giving birth
A catalyst to kiss the earth
Then take a bite from all I find
I don't invite, I'm just in time
I'll cross the circle, nought the line
I'll boss the hurdle, thought the mind

I am the sadness of the land
And from the madness of the man
And in his method was my plan
To make a leopard, understand
That I am nothing without you
I am the heartstring of the fool
I'll leave him broken, torn and threw
Into the thorns the roses grew

I cause disaster, hurt and pain
I chill the ice and burn the flame
I'll take the eyesight of the lame
I'll snap the crutch and shake the brain
I come in many shapes and form
I'll be the thunder in the storm
I'll be the well where tears are drawn
I'll be the hell where fears are born

I'll be the all you think you need
I'll be the reason why you greed
I'll make you want me till you bleed
I'll make you hunt me then I'll lead
You to the deepest, darkest night
I'll give you black and paint it white
I'll dig a hole and pick a fight
And if I win, you lose all rights

I can't do nothing by myself
I'm like a book that's on a shelf
If you refuse me, I will wither
If you choose me, I will live
I can be used in many ways
I don't have views, I don't give praise
I'm not a greeting, guide or stranger
My receipt's inside the changer'

Prune Dent

I am nailed, bonded and bailed
Sale; to a ship, whipped till I wailed

I am loose; fruit full of juice
Drained till I'm dry, still a prune has its use

I am fed, food for the dead
So many have fought, for their front lines my head

I am sharp, blacker than dark
Scarred deep for life, still there's love in my heart

I am bold! Heaven be hold
Rocky, so rocky, this road paved with gold

I am real, touch me I feel
My tongue is a knife, still my words come to heal

I can write, wrongs in the fight
And giving the reasons and ways to unite

Inscript strict non-fiction, the keeper is back
With deepest conviction, and deeper impact

Give And Take

Give me the knowledge I must understand
Show me the path of the born son of man
Give me the love that you force into hate
Give me the world our true God did create
Take back your anger, your conflict and war
Take back the misery, pain of the poor
Take back your weapons, your drugs, and your greed
Take back your vultures, there's nothing to feed

Give back the earth what you take from the soil
Give back the forest and give back the oil
Give back the innocence you turn to sin
Give back to nature, and feel it within
Give back the children you slew as you played
Give back the continents that you invade
Give back the people what's rightfully theirs
Give back their freedom and take back their fears

Give back the dignity; take back your pride
Take back your evil it kills them inside
Take back your promises, all of them too
For they are false and you are not true
Take back missionaries sent to deceive
Angels of darkness, Venus's thieves
Take back your temples where worship is done
In the name of the father, but not the right one

Take back your demons that dwell in our day
Take back your spirits, they go the wrong way
Take back your wickedness, you won't survive
For you choose the death instead of the life
Give back the scriptures you hide behind doors
Give back the commandments; take back your order
Give back the food you keep in the field
Give back all of the lives you have killed

Take back your slavery, take back your chain
Take back your burdens, the sorrow, the shame
Give back our prophets you murdered to silence
Give back the peace and take back the violence
Give back the unity, give back the justice
Give back the honesty so they can trust this
Give back the hope you stole from the soul
Give back the power you use to control

Take back your system, it's corrupt right through
Take back your torture, your actions are cruel
Take back your lies they defy what is good
Give back the truth and give back brotherhood
Give back the mothers that you watered down
Give back the motherland; the sacred ground
Give back the praise you deny the most high
Give back the love, give back then die

Tunnel Visionary

If love murdered hate
Would that make her bad?
If hate murdered love
Would anger be glad?
If anger was calm
Would rainbow and storm
Surrender each arm;
As a star child is corm

If I had a pound
And told you to weight
And balance your sound
Your reward won't be late
Would you stand up strong?
Or would you be vex?
Stand under or long
You're surrounding apex

If love was a gun
And blew through your head
Would thinking be fun
Or would feeling be dead?
If spirit was power
And power was free
Would man, child and hour
Be prison or key?

If you was a dove
Would you soar the sky
And drop down your stool
On a fool, as you fly?
Or would you be humble?
Or fly like a dream;
The cookie can crumble
In concrete or cream

If you were a cat
If you had her eyes
With green gold in black
In a personal prize
If kittens were born
And a dog at your door
Said they must be torn
From your side and amour

Would you give them free?
Would you give them free?
Or tell him to go
For you know all mighty
Or would you run yonder;
Through fear and from harm?
Or would you stand stronger
And ring the Alarm?

If love murdered hate
Would that make her bad?
And if she was happy
Would happy be sad?
If love was a mission
In tunnels of light
I'd tell you a vision;
The Fewture is bright!

Good Knight

What do you do when you steer right
Into the eyes of death;
Dark knight in the day?

What do you do when you stare right
Into what is left?
Love me any way

What do you do when you steer right
In the sight
Of all that you can't see?

If only you knew, you would turn right into
The all
That you can be

Prophets See

The stars are as the prophets in the womb
Even with eyes closed;
Their sight is open
Even as they grow;
Their destiny fulfilled
And the blinded pupil;
Brighter than the sun
Wiser than that!
See in, even more than out
And one with every corner;
Centred with the heart from the beginning
Needing not even a feeble excuse to sound;
Around before ears
Could give him, and receive...

And as the clock strikes nine
Three more heads are chosen;
And order in them still
And they move as the season
And named accordingly
For reason follows;
His feet are lighter than air
Peace; full in the chaos
Only his voice; to be heard in silence

And if I lie;
Lightening strike the same man
Ten times!
In the same place;
(Even as it carries him there)!

For truth is like the very seed
That grows into a tree;
His roots can nigh be severed
Nor pulled from his place
For this is hidden
And deeper than the depths of all the seas
Even than that of the skies within his sphere;
And his spirit be on the tongue
Even in the blink of the I

For a lie is like the very weeds
To grow in his garden
Scattered 'mong the seed;
Their deep is superficial
Not even knowing his time,
And theirs is limited –with reason;
And his hand snatch'eth them away
Like a ripe apple
From a tree that will always produce
 –But they do wither and die

For truth be the only one standing
In the hurricane's storm;
For he was born in peace and always calm
And he does bless his seed
With the mighty of many
And they does grow like the strands of here
From his very head,
Yea' his mouth the very space;
He speaks planets!
As for his eyes;
The stars extremely in their stead

Be Loved

And I was hurt
And I was hurt
And I was stamped
And in the dirt
And I was watered
By the reign
And I was born
And all again

And I was healed
And I was healed
And I was soft
When way was steeled
And though I cried
And I was shoved
It ain't denied
The bee was loved

Shadows

I stepped in the shadows
And two souls sunk as one
I slept in the shadows
And dreamed under the sun

Second Away

I did not want to go
Something pulled me yonder
Force in me to show
There's nothing I am fonder

I did not want to leave
Something pulled me hither
Could it be that these
Sweet petals wilt nor wither?

And you the man to hold
When flowers do surrender
And growing in the cold;
What warmth when sowing tender

A day that's such like this
As love to be the victor;
Not one who could resist
To paint a pretty picture

And shades of heaven's skies
And beauty fill a dawn in
The softness of his sighs
As wonders feel a morning

And I am what I am
And I have come so far
And you a superman;
A shining, in a star…

A split

A second be eternity for the thirst come again
And deserts parched; none like this
For from my eyes not even waterfalls
And winters freeze in heats unbearable
Gaze;
To fix upon a broken thing
Sleeping stares within
And how this limbo tears me even more
To find the key no longer fits the door
And stuck
Out
Side in the cold
Peering through steamed windows;
Dry to the touch
And stronger than steel
And me, myself
Closer than the very breath
Yet further than the stars that shine on death;
Pre-
Tending
No one's home

Nay-Ture

Winter has taken set
And my nature has seasons
They love me and yet
For different reasons
I can not explain
Or even decipher
They call out my name
They question my life

My flame has grown cold
In flicker so deep
I cry in the fold
And hardly can keep
My conscience concealed
It runs off and hither
To do as I willed
To stand and deliver

I laugh in the day;
A horse in my tone
He gallops away
In the wilderness roam
A far from a stray
So long did I enter;
A lay by the hay
In song for Amenta

At Least

And on such a night like this
Who there travels in the mist?
Winters into summer, chill
Cast-aways, in chains of steel

And from your ships, with whitest sails
You came with gifts, and praise, and hails
You left with even greater deed
And stolen from the chosen seed

You broke our necks, you bent our backs
You took away the smallest axe
You took our names, our claims, and trust
And crumbled one and all to dust

You took the womb; you raped the seed
Fulfilled your want and killed the need
You'd roast a man who broke your rule;
His mother, father, sister too!

You wipe out nations, just for fun
With just one finger, one button
You're tapping people like a pipe
How long until the chip to swipe?

You want our blood, you want our flesh
You want our piece and happiness
For you are spoilt; a spiteful child
Your nature lost, your nature wild

You boast of places you have been
Reality; a nightmare scene
You stole the sheep you led astray
Then blocked their each and every way

You are a knight; your armour pale
You speak of heaven, act like hell
You're in the world, you're on the stage
Your chaos loose, your devils rage

Your eyes, your mouth, your hands deny;
Your inner soul did fade and die
You needed life, you needed quick;
Into my heart, I felt you rip

No more! No more! No more! Forsooth
For pure hew oar, a boat of truth;
There is no captain, with no hat
No pirates looking to attack

There is no white! There is no white!
No gifts, no praises from this night
That look at us and call us beast;
Much more than you we are at least

Good – Even In

I am as the moon;
Even as I show you part – I am whole
I am as the sun;
Even as I beat the heart – I am soul
I am as the mist;
Even as I steam the skies of your pain
I am as of this;
Even as a queen – they rise in reign

I am as the star;
Even as I delve in deep – I am here
I am as the Ka;
Even as the keys I keep – stand in sphere
I am as the light;
Even in the dense of dark – sense is strong
Good day to you night
Even out of sight; I'm still, not gone

Lesson in Love

Now I go back, where the memories flood
With the sharp of the knife and the red of the blood
With the bruise from the brute, when the fist comes like led
When effused from our root we lament for the dead
And the rope for the neck, and the tree for the rope
And the after effect when we swing without hope
And the mothers are crying, the children are left
There ain't no denying, relying on death

The whip is a river; it flows through the skin
To journey beyond to the scars deep within
My claim is a mountain I never could climb
My pain is a fountain to cleanse the divine
I have seen with my eyes, death it creeps like the master
Who searches for slaves, who have fled from disaster;
We stoop in the field, we stoop deep inside
Awaiting escape, but how long can we hide

I dream of the time when the sun shone its light
And did not deny that its mother was night
And did not deny who was first to begin
From the seeds of a man to the glory of kings
To the peaks of the pyramids, aligned with the stars
We travelled the continents near and afar
We mastered philosophies, cosmologies too;
All this from a race that was darker than blue

We nurtured; each nation just willing to learn
Yet knew in our hearts that the tables would turn
Up-lifted them all with a true revelation
And deep in this guise, lost a civilisation
The teacher a pupil, the teacher a slave
The preacher can reach yah, but whom can he save?
Think of the babies, so deep in the womb;
Blacker than night, with the light of the moon

Is it too late for me? Am I cut far too deep?
There's no way to erase all the memories I keep
But not late for the children; they still have a chance
And to this vicious music they don't have to dance
With all of this suffering we have been through
Show them a way that is blessed and true
Enough of this war! Enough of this pain!
Enough of this dying and crying in vain!

No more of this wickedness; stop now this sin!
Don't look at a child as a colour of skin;
Look at the innocence deep in their eyes
For there you find purity, sacred and wise
Look at their smiles, look if you care
Beauty gets beautiful, more with the year
Look at their tears and their fears, if you're blind
Remember their cries, as you leave them behind

Please stop this agony, open your heart
Cupid is throwing a poisonous dart
Look at this system, imperial not;
Imperial stole all imperial got
Now to seek justice, not to cast blame
It's time to put out this notorious flame
'Cause we're losing our souls, we're losing our minds
We're losing controls with no conscience to find

Look at the consequence, all that's been done
All this so intense, and still more to come
A ship can not hold the release of the seas
And a life can't be sold; it is free as the breeze
Lord please have mercy, please for us all
From the wickedest man, to the child who can't crawl
Lord, please have mercy, Heavens above
If we must learn anything, let it be love

Love

What is love?
Can you make love?
Can you fake love?

I know a man who made love from clay
And over the years he watched it decay
Then he decided to make love from ice
It melted to water and flowed through his life

Then he decided to make love from stone
It's solid and strong; I'll call it my home
But it was empty, colourless, still
Love can't be made; it is something you feel

Something you need, something you know
Something you give, take, reveal and follow
Yes you can use it to move you and soothe you
Love is like music you get down and groove to;

Music so good it touches your soul
Music so real it helps you to grow
Music so strong, but you'll never see
The sound from the instruments that you set free

Oh but you know, you know that it's there
You know what you feel. You know what you hear
You know it is true when you just can't resist
You know that in you there is love just like this

I Feel No Hate

I feel no hate; there's only love
I'm feeling great, thank God above
If it turns out that he's not there
I feel no hate; I feel no fear
I am not red. I am not blue
It's like I said, I'm part of you
And if you hurt or bring me pain
I'm like a seed; I start again

I'm like a wall. I'm like a fence
I will not fall; I'm not intense
My natural state's a sonic key
And I relate with harmonically
I feel no hate; they hit me hard
Yet I'm a gate that angels guard
I open joy and happiness
I need no more than angels bless

I feel no hate; there's only peace
I feel at one with my release
I'm with the light; The light of truth
And my insight will stand as proof
I'll prove to you that life is free
And what you choose; that you shall be
You ask me how; you're in the mist
I'm here, I'm now; I'm just like this

I live and learn, I ain't a saint
I show concern. I show restraint
I have my roots; I'm like a tree
My words are fruits; I'm energy
I balance night; I balance day
I hold them tight; I'm just that way
For opposites born of the same
As waters lit the fires flame

The sky reflects the seven seas
The earth protects the birds and bees
The thought digests within the mind
And I profess with human kind
The kind nest grows for those who fly
The flower's rose within the eye
Imagination gives you wings
With revelations caged birds sing

I feel no hate, there's only strength
And I create with inner sense
I will not judge, I'm full of range
I will not budge, yet all ways change
And all that grows is living too
My rain bows flow and interview
The sun shines out with touching rays
I'm all about; I'm in a maze

A maze in grace, a maze in mind
Amazing feelings here to find
I feel no fear; I take control
Don't shed a tear, I feel your soul
I feel the world; I know the land
I feel no hate; I understand
I feel each move; I feel each turn
Each tree, each groove, each water's burn

I feel no hate; I only love
Inspired by the Eagle's dove
For I am one and also free
I come in from eternity
I feel afloat; I take a flight
No ship, no boat, just high of height
I feel no hate; my heart is true
For as day breaks; it heals anew

En-Capture

You're like the atmosphere;
I need you to survive
But I could never capture you

All around me; even within
Still,
I could never capture you

In a picture maybe;
Beautiful and majestic
With all the honours expression can allow
There I could glimpse
(Maybe in reflection);
Your profound
Elusive
In Surrection

But never capture
No,
I could never capture you

Step Inside

Step in the tunnel, feel no fear
With each step you take your freedom is near
Don't be afraid, there's light at the end
Go through with courage, walk on my friend
One side is night time, and one side is day
One side will give love and one take away
You stand in limbo, you stand between
The shadows of tunnels within your own being
Go through the tunnel, go through the dark
Go to the power that's deep in your heart
Walk through with dignity, walk through with pride
Come to your destiny, come step inside

God in Disguise

I met a man on a winding road
A humble man with a heart of gold
He had a vision of unity
He was on a mission to destiny

He said, 'From yonder do I come
I bear no weapon, just my tongue
I speak the truth, I tell no lie
I give a love that can not die'

I met an angel, I'm telling you it's true
With skies in the eyes of the sweet morning dew
With wings light as stars, watched him shine in the air
He walked upon waters and washed away fear

Moon in his hands, stars in his eyes
Born son of man; God in this guise
Moon in his hands, stars in his eyes
Ruler of man, God in disguise

The Way We War

The way we war
It breaks my heart
And peace is tore
From never part
The way you chance
Your love and life
And spirits dance
In sacrifice

The way you sin
The way you shout
The way is in
You throw it out
The way you talk
And slander deep
The way you walk;
You should retreat

The way you turn
The way you bend
The way you burn
And never mend
The way you strike
Your brother down
The way you stand
A stolen crown

The way you teach!
The way you teach!
The dirt! The hurt
The out of reach
The blinded from
The light I shine
Reminded come
The child is mine

The child is real!
The child is real!
The child is touching
Where I feel
And now I watch
The children die
And still, you do not
See me cry

But cry I do!
But cry I do!
For man and child
And woman too
And tears of oceans
For the lamb
And sheer devotion
Where I am

And angels wings
And angels wings
And stars of angels
Guide all things
And stars of heaven
Crown all nights
They stand in seven
Frown in fights

And I am mad
And I am just
And I am sad
And still I trust
And I have never
Banished claim
And still you cry
And not my name

And still you die
And still you die
And still you die
And ask me why
And still you doubt
And sheep are heard
And still you shout
And born a bird

And vultures spy
And vultures swoop
And baby bird's
Asleep in coop
And still I give
You power free
To conquer all
Who turn from me

For I am mad!
For I am mad!
For I am good
And never bad
For I have watched
My paradise
Be brained and washed
Like tainted rice

And you must see
And you must see
And you must open
Up to thee
And you must know
I'm sending down
And you must grow
And all a round

And you must give
Yes, you must give
And you must know
The life to live
And you must take it
Consciously
For I can sub
Marine and see

The way we war
It breaks my heart
Still I am sure
As of the start
I love you more
As day return;
And eye a door
The few who learn

The butterfly and the Bee

The butterfly said to the bee
'Why you are far sweeter than me'
The bee said in return
"It's your freedom of life that I yearn"
The butterfly said in reply
'No you are far more free than I
But you can always return home
And there you are never alone'

Name one thing you can't think of…